Social Security Made Simple

Social Security Retirement Benefits and
Related Planning Topics
Explained in 100 Pages or Less

Social Security
Made Simple

Social Security Retirement Benefits and
Related Planning Topics
Explained in 100 Pages or Less

Mike Piper

Simple Subjects, LLC
St. Louis, Missouri, 63110
ISBN: 978-0-9814542-8-3
www.ObliviousInvestor.com

Dedication

For you, the reader, so that you can get the benefits you deserve from the system you've spent so many years paying into.

Why is there a light bulb on the cover?

In cartoons and comics, a light bulb is often used to signify a moment of clarity or sudden understanding—an "aha!" moment. My hope is that the books in the ...*in 100 Pages or Less* series can help readers achieve clarity and understanding of topics that are often considered complex and confusing—hence the light bulb.

Disclaimer

This text is intended to be an introduction to some of the Social Security topics that are most likely to play a role in your retirement planning. It is *not*, however, intended to be a substitute for personalized advice from a professional advisor. The author will make his best effort to keep the information current and accurate; however, given the ever-changing nature of the subject matter, no guarantee can be made as to the accuracy of the information contained within.

The text includes information about some of the tax consequences of Social Security benefits. While nothing contained within should be construed as tax advice, any tax-related information is not intended or written to be used, and cannot be used, for the purpose of avoiding penalties under the Internal Revenue Code or promoting, marketing, or recommending to another party any transaction or matter addressed in this book.

Your Feedback Is Appreciated!

As the author of this book, I'm very interested to hear your thoughts. If you find the book helpful, please let me know! Alternatively, if you have any suggestions of ways to make the book better, I'm eager to hear that, too.

Finally, if you're unsatisfied with your purchase for any reason, let me know, and I'll be happy to provide you with a refund of the current list price of the book (limited to one refund per household).

You can reach me at: mike@simplesubjects.com.

Best Regards,
Mike Piper, CPA

Table of Contents

Part Two
Rules for Less Common Situations

Part Three
Social Security Planning:
When to Claim Benefits

Part Four
Other Related Planning Topics

INTRODUCTION

The Benefits of Understanding Your Benefits

According to the Social Security Administration, as of 2012, Social Security benefits make up approximately 39% of the income of U.S. citizens age 65 or older. Unfortunately, it's common for retirees to make decisions regarding their Social Security benefits that cause them to miss out on tens of thousands of dollars (or sometimes even hundreds of thousands of dollars) over the course of their retirement.

Assuming that you anticipate Social Security benefits playing a meaningful role in your retirement finances, it's important for you to understand how the system works and what you can do to get the most out of your benefits.

What We'll Be Covering

This book is organized into four sections. Part 1 covers the basic rules: how retirement benefits are calculated, how spousal benefits are calculated, and how widow(er) benefits are calculated. Part 2 takes a look at the rules for a handful of slightly less common situations—when you or your spouse have a pension from government work, for instance. Part 3 discusses the question of when to start taking Social Security benefits and provides a few strategies for getting the most out of your benefits. Part 4 covers some related planning topics such as tax planning opportunities that arise as a result of the unique way in which Social Security benefits are taxed.

But Won't the Rules Change?

When Social Security was first created, it covered a much smaller group of workers; it did not provide for spousal benefits or widow(er) benefits; it did not allow for retirement benefits prior to age 65; and benefits weren't subject to federal income tax at all. In other words, Social Security originally looked quite different than it looks today.

Similarly, it's likely that the Social Security system will continue to evolve in the future. Of course, there's no way to know when the rules will change, for whom they will change, or what those changes will be. So, for lack of any other reasonable option, this book is written based on the rules as they stand now.

If, however, you're working on your retirement plan and you're intent on making some sort of downward adjustment to your projected Social Security benefits to account for the program's financial troubles, the 2012 Social Security Trustees Report may be of use.[1] The report projected that there will be sufficient funds to cover 100% of benefits promised under the current system up until 2033, at which point there will only be enough money to pay for approximately 75% of projected benefits. Does that mean that benefits will go unchanged for the next twenty years, then drop across the board, all at once, by 25%? Probably not. What actually *will* happen? Your guess is as good as mine.

Let's Keep This Brief

As with the other books in the *...in 100 Pages or Less* series, the goal of this book is a modest one: to provide an introduction to the aspects of Social Security that are most likely to factor into your retirement planning. In other words, this book is *not* intended to turn you into a Social Security expert. Nor is it intended to serve as a 100%-comprehensive guide to every aspect of Social Security.[2]

---

[1] The report is available at:
http://www.ssa.gov/oact/tr/2012/tr2012.pdf
[2] For example, disability-related benefits are not covered in this book at all. If you're interested in an understandable book that *does* cover those benefits, I'd suggest reading *Social Security: The Inside Story* by Andy Landis.

PART ONE

Social Security Basics

CHAPTER ONE

Qualifying for Retirement Benefits

To qualify for Social Security retirement benefits, you must:

1. Be age 62 or older, and
2. Have earned 40 Social Security "credits" over the course of your career. [1]

Attaining Age 62

The first month for which you can receive a benefit payment is the first month in which you are age 62 for the entire month. This means that, for most people, the first month for which you can receive

---

[1] If you become disabled prior to age 62, it's possible to qualify for retirement benefits with fewer than 40 credits.

benefits is the month *after* the month including your 62nd birthday. If, however, your 62nd birthday is on the first or second day of the month, you are considered to be age 62 for that entire month.

Earning Social Security Credits

Social Security credits are earned by working at a job where you pay Social Security taxes or by earning money from self-employment. The amount of earnings needed to earn a credit is adjusted each year in keeping with wage inflation. For 2012, you receive one credit for each $1,130 of covered income that you earn during the year.

Credits are sometimes called "quarters of coverage" because you can earn a maximum of four per year. To earn four credits in a given year, however, you do not actually have to work in each of the four calendar quarters. For instance, if you earned $4,520 in January of 2012 and did not work for the rest of the year, you would still earn four credits for the year.

Chapter 1 Simple Summary

- Unless you become disabled prior to age 62, in order to qualify for Social Security retirement benefits you must be 62 years old, and you must have earned at least 40 "credits."

- You can earn a maximum of four Social Security credits per year.

- In 2012, you earn one Social Security credit for each $1,130 of income you earn that is subject to Social Security taxes.

CHAPTER TWO

How Retirement Benefits Are Calculated

The size of your monthly retirement benefit depends on:

1. Your earnings history, and
2. How old you are when you first begin taking benefits. [1]

But first we need to back up a step. In order to understand how Social Security benefits are calculated, you need to be familiar with two terms:

- "full retirement age" (FRA), and
- "primary insurance amount" (PIA).

---

[1] It can depend on other factors as well, such as your current earnings if you have a job while you're collecting Social Security. But for simplicity's sake, let's start with the most basic scenario.

Your full retirement age depends on the year in which you were born (see table below). Your primary insurance amount is the amount of retirement benefits you would receive per month if you started taking them at your full retirement age. As we'll discuss shortly, your PIA is determined by your earnings history.

Year of Birth[1]	Full Retirement Age
1937 or earlier	65
1938	65 and 2 months
1939	65 and 4 months
1940	65 and 6 months
1941	65 and 8 months
1942	65 and 10 months
1943-1954	66
1955	66 and 2 months
1956	66 and 4 months
1957	66 and 6 months
1958	66 and 8 months
1959	66 and 10 months
1960 or later	67

---

[1] If your birthday is January 1st, you will be treated as if you were born in the prior year for the purpose of determining your full retirement age.

arnings History Affects Retirement Benefits

Your primary insurance amount is based on your historical earnings. Specifically, it's based on your "average indexed monthly earnings" (AIME). Calculating your AIME is a four-step process.

1. Adjust your earnings from prior years to today's dollars.[1]
2. Select your 35 highest-earning years.
3. Add up the total amount of earnings in those 35 years, excluding any earnings for each year that were in excess of the maximum amount subject to Social Security tax.[2]
4. Divide by 420 (the number of months in 35 years).

You do not actually have to do this calculation yourself. The Social Security Administration does it for you. It is, however, important to understand the

---

[1] Specifically, earnings from years prior to the year in which you reach age 60 are adjusted for the growth in the national average wage that occurred between the year in which you earned the money and the year in which you reached age 60. Earnings from years after you reach age 60 are included in the calculation at their actual dollar amount.

[2] For historical maximums by year, see: http://www.socialsecurity.gov/planners/maxtax.htm

concept, so that you can understand how your benefit is calculated.

Calculating Your Primary Insurance Amount

For someone becoming eligible for retirement benefits (that is, reaching age 62) in 2012, his or her primary insurance amount would be:

- 90% of any AIME up to $767, plus
- 32% of any AIME between $767 and $4,624, plus
- 15% of any AIME above $4,624.[1]

Or, to put it in terms of annual income, if claimed at full retirement age, Social Security would replace:

- 90% of the first $9,204 of average annual wage-inflation-adjusted earnings, plus
- 32% of average annual wage-inflation-adjusted earnings from $9,205 to $55,488, plus
- 15% of average annual wage-inflation-adjusted earnings from $55,489 to $98,388.

---

[1] These figures change to account for wage inflation each year. So, for example, for somebody turning age 62 in 2013, each of these dollar amounts will probably be slightly higher.

Two noteworthy takeaways here are that:

1. Social Security replaces a higher portion of wages for lower-earning workers than for higher-earning workers, and
2. There's a maximum possible Social Security retirement benefit. (Few people reach that maximum though, because doing so would require that you earn the maximum earnings subject to Social Security tax for 35 different years.)

If You Worked Fewer than 35 Years

If you have fewer than 35 years in which you earned income subject to Social Security taxes, the calculation of your average indexed monthly earnings will include zeros. For example, if you worked for 31 years, your AIME calculation would include those 31 years of earnings, as well as 4 years of zeros.

As a result, working additional years would result in those zero-earnings years being knocked out of the calculation and replaced with your current earnings. The result isn't going to make you rich, but it's worth including in your list of considerations when deciding when to retire.

How Age Affects Retirement Benefits

If you wait until *after* full retirement age to claim your retirement benefit, the amount you receive will be greater than your primary insurance amount. For anybody born in 1943 or later, the increase is $2/3$ of 1% for each month you wait beyond full retirement age (up to age 70, beyond which there is no increase for waiting). This works out to an increase of 8% per year.[1]

EXAMPLE: Alan was born in 1954, so his full retirement age is 66. His primary insurance amount is $2,000. If he waits until age 70 (that is, 48 months after FRA) to claim his retirement benefit, he will receive $2,640 per month, calculated as:

- His PIA of $2,000 per month, plus
- $2/3$ of 1% x 48 months x $2,000.

If you claim your retirement benefit *prior* to full retirement age, it will be reduced from your primary insurance amount by $5/9$ of 1% for each month (up to 36 months) prior to full retirement age. This works out to a reduction of 6.67% per year. For each month in excess of 36 months, the reduction is $5/12$ of 1% (or 5% per year).

---

[1] The monthly rates of increase for people born prior to 1943 can be found at:
http://www.socialsecurity.gov/retire2/delayret.htm

EXAMPLE: Allison was born in 1950, so her full retirement age is 66. Her primary insurance amount is $2,000. If she claims retirement benefits at age 64 (24 months prior to FRA), her monthly benefit would be $1,733.33, calculated as:

- Her PIA of $2,000 per month, minus
- $5/9$ of 1% x 24 months x $2,000.[1]

If Allison instead decided to claim as early as possible, at age 62 (48 months prior to FRA), her benefit would be $1,500 per month, calculated as:

- Her PIA of $2,000 per month, minus
- $5/9$ of 1% x 36 months x $2,000, minus
- $5/12$ of 1% x 12 months x $2,000.

In short, the interaction between the size of your retirement benefits and the age at which you first claim that benefit looks like this:

---

[1] Allison would actually receive $1,733 per month, because the Social Security Administration rounds all monthly benefit payments *down* to the next lower multiple of $1.

Age when you claim retirement benefits	Amount of retirement benefit[1]
5 years before FRA	70% of PIA
4 years before FRA	75% of PIA
3 years before FRA	80% of PIA
2 years before FRA	86.67% of PIA
1 year before FRA	93.33% of PIA
at FRA	100% of PIA
1 year after FRA	108% of PIA
2 years after FRA	116% of PIA
3 years after FRA	124% of PIA
4 years after FRA	132% of PIA

Adjusting Benefits for Inflation

Every year after you become eligible for benefits, your primary insurance amount is adjusted to keep up with inflation as measured by the Consumer Price Index for Urban Wage Earners and Clerical Workers (CPI-W). When your PIA is adjusted upward for inflation, it increases not only your retirement

---

[1] Please note that the increases and decreases are actually based on *months* before or after full retirement age, rather than years. So the actual amount you receive will probably be between two of the figures listed in this table. In addition, as mentioned above, the actual formulas use fractions rather than decimals, which could result in slightly different amounts.

11

benefit, but also any other benefits that are based on your PIA (e.g., your spouse's spousal benefits and/or widow/widower benefits if your spouse should outlive you).[1]

For brevity's sake, I will be writing in "today's dollars" throughout this book. In other words, rather than explicitly mentioning in nearly every single paragraph that the benefit(s) discussed would be adjusted for inflation, I will simply write what the benefit would be, as measured today. Please understand that, from there, the benefit would be adjusted annually in keeping with inflation.

---

[1] Contrary to a common misconception, CPI-W *does* account for changes in the prices of food and energy.

Chapter 2 Simple Summary

- Your "primary insurance amount" (PIA) is the monthly retirement benefit you would receive if you claimed benefits at "full retirement age" (FRA).

- Your primary insurance amount is calculated based on your 35 highest-earning years (after adjusting prior years' earnings for wage inflation).

- If you claim retirement benefits prior to your full retirement age, you will receive an amount smaller than your PIA. If you wait until after your full retirement age to claim benefits, your retirement benefit will be greater than your PIA.

- Social Security benefits are adjusted on an annual basis to keep up with inflation (as measured by the CPI-W).

CHAPTER THREE

Spousal Social Security Benefits

Upon reaching age 62, even if you have no work history of your own, you can begin receiving a Social Security benefit as the spouse of somebody who is entitled to a retirement or disability benefit, provided that you meet one of three requirements:

1. You have been married to your spouse for at least one year,
2. You, together with your spouse, are the natural parent of a child, or
3. In the month before you married your current spouse, you were eligible to collect a widow(er) benefit or a spousal benefit based on another spouse's work record.

If you are not yet age 62, you can receive a spousal benefit if you meet the other applicable requirements and you have in your care a child who is entitled to child's benefits on your spouse's record (which we'll discuss in Chapter 6) and who is under age 16 or disabled.

It's important to note that you cannot claim spousal benefits until your spouse has filed for his/her own retirement benefit. However, if your spouse has reached full retirement age, he/she can file for benefits and immediately ask to have the payments suspended, thereby allowing the amount to continue to grow as if he/she had not yet filed. (This is known as the "file and suspend" strategy, and we'll discuss it more thoroughly in Chapter 11.)

In addition, you cannot claim spousal Social Security benefits if you have filed for your own retirement benefit and your own primary insurance amount is greater than one-half of your spouse's primary insurance amount.

Filing for Spousal Benefits after Full Retirement Age

If you wait until full retirement age to begin collecting spousal benefits, and you are not receiving a retirement benefit based on your own work record, your spousal benefit will be equal to 50% of your spouse's primary insurance amount.[1] Unlike retire-

---

[1] As we'll discuss in Chapters 6 and 7 your spousal benefit could potentially be reduced as a result of the family maximum if other people are also claiming bene-

ment benefits, spousal benefits are not increased by waiting beyond full retirement age to claim them.

EXAMPLE: Lydia's primary insurance amount is $1,800. If her husband Carl has no work record of his own and he claims spousal benefits at or after full retirement age, he would receive 50% of Lydia's PIA, or $900 per month.

Filing for Spousal Benefits prior to Full Retirement Age

If you claim spousal benefits prior to full retirement age, your spousal benefit will be reduced as a function of how many months early you claimed. The reduction will be $25/_{36}$ of 1% for each month early, up to 36 months. For each month in excess of 36 months, the reduction is $5/_{12}$ of 1%. Translate that into years, and you get the following table:

If you claim spousal benefits...	You will receive:
At full retirement age	100% of spousal benefit
1 year prior to FRA	91.67% of spousal benefit
2 years prior to FRA	83.33% of spousal benefit
3 years prior to FRA	75% of spousal benefit
4 years prior to FRA	70% of spousal benefit
5 years prior to FRA	65% of spousal benefit

fits on your spouse's work record or as a result of the Government Pension Offset if you receive a pension.

EXAMPLE: Nadia is not eligible for benefit of her own. Her husband Tir primary insurance amount of $1,40 claims her spousal benefit three years prior to reaching full retirement age, she will receive $525 per month, calculated as 75% of 50% of her husband's $1,400 PIA.

Spousal Benefits with Retirement Benefits

If you file for spousal benefits at the same time you are receiving a retirement benefit of your own, the total amount you receive is a function of how your PIA compares to your spouse's PIA.

Specifically, your spousal benefit will be calculated as:

Reduction factor (from previous table) x 50% of your spouse's PIA, minus your PIA

Your own retirement benefit will then be added to your spousal benefit to determine the total amount you'll receive.

EXAMPLE: Catherine's primary insurance amount is $700. Her husband Michael's primary insurance amount is $1,600. If Catherine files for spousal benefits and her own retirement benefit four years prior to full retirement age, the total amount she will receive is $595, calculated as follows:

- Catherine's own benefit of $525, calculated as $700 x 75% (due to claiming four years prior to FRA), plus
- Catherine's spousal benefit of $70, calculated as:

70% (from previous table)   x   [(50% x 1,600) − 700]

A spousal benefit cannot, however, be negative. So, in the event that a person's spousal benefit calculation would yield a negative result (which would happen any time a person's own PIA is greater than 50% of his/her spouse's PIA), that person would receive his/her own retirement benefit and no spousal benefit.

EXAMPLE: Heather's primary insurance amount is $1,400. Her husband George's primary insurance amount is $1,500. If Heather files for her own benefit and spousal benefits, she'll simply receive her own benefit, because her PIA is greater than 50% of George's PIA.

It's also important to understand that if you are eligible for spousal benefits and for your own retirement benefit, and you file for either of the two prior to reaching full retirement age, you will be "deemed" to have filed for the other type of benefit as well. The purpose of this rule is to prevent you from being able to file for only one type of benefit, while allowing the other benefit to continue to grow.

If, however, you have reached full retirement age, you can file for just your spousal benefit by filing what's known as a "restricted application," thereby allowing your own retirement benefit to continue growing until age 70. We'll discuss this more thoroughly in Chapter 11.

EXAMPLE: Earl's full retirement age is 66. At age 64, he files for a spousal benefit on his wife's earnings record. As a result, he's deemed to have filed for his own retirement benefit as well.

If Earl had waited until age 66, he could file a "restricted application" for spousal benefits only. If he did so, his own retirement benefit could continue to grow until age 70.

Chapter 3 Simple Summary

- If you claim spousal benefits at (or after) full retirement age, your spousal benefit will be equal to the difference between 50% of your spouse's primary insurance amount and your own primary insurance amount. (Therefore, if you have no retirement benefit of your own, you will receive 50% of your spouse's PIA.)

- If you claim spousal benefits prior to full retirement age, the amount you receive per month will be permanently reduced.

- In most cases, the youngest age at which you can qualify for spousal benefits is 62.

- If you are eligible for both spousal benefits and your own retirement benefit, and you claim either one prior to full retirement age, you will be deemed to have filed for the other benefit as well.

CHAPTER FOUR

Widow(er) Social Security Benefits

If you are a widow or widower, you may be able to claim a widow(er) benefit based on your deceased spouse's work record. In most cases, in order to be eligible for widow(er) benefits:

- The marriage must have lasted at least nine months,
- You must be at least 60 years old (or disabled and at least age 50),
- You must not have remarried, unless you re-married *after* reaching age 60, and
- Your spouse must have been "fully insured" at the time of his/her death.[1]

---

[1] For exceptions to these three general requirements, see section 404.335 of the Code of Federal Regulations, available at:
http://www.ssa.gov/OP_Home/cfr20/404/404-0335.htm

To be fully insured, your spouse must have earned a number of Social Security credits equal to his/her age at the time of death, minus 22, subject to two exceptions:

1. If your spouse died prior to age 28, six credits are required for fully insured status, and
2. No more than 40 credits are required, even if your spouse was older than 62 at the time of his/her death.

Calculation of Widow(er) Benefits

The amount of the widow(er) benefit will be 100% of the deceased spouse's primary insurance amount if:

- The deceased spouse was younger than full retirement age and had not yet filed for benefits, and
- The surviving spouse claims widow(er) benefits at or after his or her own full retirement age.

If the deceased spouse had claimed benefits earlier than FRA, the surviving spouse's widow(er) benefit, rather than being based on the deceased spouse's PIA, will be based on the *larger* of:

- The amount that the deceased spouse was receiving, or

- 82.5% of the deceased spouse's primary insurance amount.

EXAMPLE: Henry has a full retirement age of 66. He claims his retirement benefits at age 63, meaning his retirement benefit is 80% of his primary insurance amount.

Henry then dies at age 65. His wife Wanda (who has already reached full retirement age) claims a widow's benefit immediately. Wanda's widow's benefit will be 82.5% of Henry's primary insurance amount (because she gets the greater of 82.5% or the amount he was receiving, which was 80%).

If the deceased spouse claimed benefits after reaching FRA, the surviving spouse's widow(er) benefit will be based on the amount that the deceased spouse was receiving.

EXAMPLE: Harry claims benefits at age 68, then dies at age 69. Harry's wife Rita (who has already reached full retirement age) claims a widow's benefit immediately. Rita's widow's benefit will be equal to the benefit that Harry had been receiving at the time of his death (which will be greater than Harry's primary insurance amount, because he claimed after full retirement age).

If the deceased spouse had reached full retirement age but had not yet filed for benefits, the surviving spouse's widow(er) benefit will be based on the amount that the deceased spouse would have received if he/she had filed on the date of his/her death.

EXAMPLE: Lynn dies at age 69, having never filed for her own retirement benefit. Lynn's husband Hank (who has already reached full retirement age) immediately claims a widower's benefit. Hank's widower's benefit will be equal to the amount that Lynn would have received if she had filed for her own benefit on her date of death.

Like retirement benefits and spousal benefits, widow(er) benefits are adjusted for inflation. This inflation adjustment includes any time between the date at which the first spouse dies and the date at which the surviving spouse claims a widow(er)'s benefit.

EXAMPLE: Wendy dies at 64, having filed for benefits at age 63. Her husband Howard is 60 years old at the time of Wendy's death. Six years later, upon reaching his full retirement age of 66, Howard files for widower benefits. He'll receive the amount that Wendy was receiving, adjusted for any inflation that occurred over the six intervening years.

Claiming Widow(er) Benefits Prior to Full Retirement Age

If the surviving spouse claims widow(er) benefits *prior* to reaching full retirement age, the amount received will be reduced. Widow(er) benefits claimed at age 60 (the minimum age for widow(er) benefits) will be equal to 71.5% of the amount that would have been received if claimed at full retirement age.[1]

EXAMPLE: June dies at age 63, having never filed for benefits. As discussed previously, this means that if her husband Frank claims his widower's benefit at full retirement age, he will receive an amount equal to June's primary insurance amount. If Frank claims at age 60, however, he will only receive 71.5% of June's primary insurance amount.

The reduction in widow(er) benefits decreases proportionately as the claimant nears full retirement age. So, for example, if the surviving spouse claims widower benefits halfway between age 60 and full retirement age, the amount received will be 85.75% (that is, halfway between 71.5% and 100%) of the amount that would have been received at FRA.

---

[1] Exception: If the deceased spouse had claimed retirement benefits prior to FRA and the surviving spouse claims widow(er) benefits prior to FRA as well, the widow(er) benefit will be greater than what the above would indicate. See Appendix A for details.

Full Retirement Age for Widow(er) Benefits

You may have a slightly different full retirement age for the purpose of calculating widow(er) benefits than you do for the purpose of calculating retirement benefits or spousal benefits. As compared to the FRA chart for retirement benefits (as shown in Chapter 2), the FRA chart for survivor benefits has each of the dates of birth shifted two years into the future, as follows:

Year of Birth[1]	Full Retirement Age for Widow(er) Benefits
1939 or earlier	65
1940	65 and 2 months
1941	65 and 4 months
1942	65 and 6 months
1943	65 and 8 months
1944	65 and 10 months
1945-1956	66
1957	66 and 2 months
1958	66 and 4 months
1959	66 and 6 months
1960	66 and 8 months
1961	66 and 10 months
1962 or later	67

---

[1] As with retirement benefits, if your birthday is January 1st, you will be treated as if you were born in the prior year for the purpose of determining your FRA.

Widow(er) Benefits Combined with Other Benefits

If a person claims widow(er) benefits at the same time that he/she is receiving a retirement benefit (or a spousal benefit) the total amount he/she receives will be the greater of the two benefit amounts.[1]

---

[1] Technically, if your widow(er) benefit is greater than your own retirement benefit, you receive your own retirement benefit, plus your widow(er) benefit, after reducing your widow(er) benefit by the amount of your own retirement benefit. As you'll notice, this generally results in you receiving an amount equal to your widow(er) benefit alone, though there are some cases where other rules come into play that make this distinction important.

Chapter 4 Simple Summary

- If you are a widow or widower and your deceased spouse earned a sufficient number of Social Security credits by the time of his/her death, you may be eligible for a widow(er) benefit based on his/her work record.

- In most cases, age 60 is the earliest date at which a person can claim widow(er) benefits.

- The amount of the widow(er) benefit you receive depends both on the date at which your deceased spouse began claiming benefits and on the date at which you begin claiming your widow(er) benefit.

PART TWO

Rules for Less Common Situations

CHAPTER FIVE

Social Security for Divorced Spouses

There are two types of benefits that can be claimed based on an ex-spouse's earnings record:

1. Divorced spouse benefits, and
2. Surviving divorced spouse benefits.

The rules for both types of benefits are quite similar to those for still-married couples.

Qualifying for Divorced Spouse Benefits

To qualify for spousal benefits on behalf of an ex-spouse's earnings record, you must:

- Have been married for at least ten years immediately before the divorce became final,

- Be age 62 or older, and
- Not currently be married.

In addition, either a) your ex-spouse must have already claimed his/her own retirement (or disability) benefit, or b) he/she must be eligible to claim such a benefit and you have been divorced for at least two years.

For the most part, divorced spouse benefits are calculated the same way as regular spousal benefits. That is, if you claim at full retirement age, your benefit as an ex-spouse will be equal to:

- 50% of your ex-spouse's primary insurance amount, minus
- Your own primary insurance amount.

Also, like regular spousal benefits:

- If you claim prior to your FRA, your divorced spouse benefit will be reduced,
- You do not get any additional benefit for waiting beyond full retirement age, and
- You cannot claim divorced spouse benefits if you have filed for your own retirement benefit and your own primary insurance amount is greater than one-half of your ex-spouse's primary insurance amount.

As with normal spousal benefits, if you claim divorced spouse benefits prior to full retirement age, you will be deemed to have filed for your own retirement benefit as well. (And conversely, if you file for your own retirement benefit prior to full retirement age, you will be deemed to have filed for your divorced spousal benefit as well.)

If, however, you wait until full retirement age to claim divorced spouse benefits, it will not be treated as filing for your own benefit—thereby allowing you to receive divorced spouse benefits for a few years while you allow your own retirement benefit to grow until age 70. (We'll discuss this strategy more thoroughly in Chapter 11.)

Qualifying for Surviving Divorced Spouse Benefits

If your ex-spouse has passed away, you may be eligible for surviving divorced spouse benefits on his or her behalf. In order to qualify:

- You must have been married for at least ten years immediately before the divorce became final,
- You must be age 60 or older (or disabled and at least age 50),
- You must not currently be married (or you remarried after reaching age 60), and
- Your ex-spouse must have been "fully insured" (as explained in Chapter 4) at the time of his/her death.

Calculating Surviving Divorced Spouse Benefits

In general, surviving divorced spouse benefits are calculated the same way as widow(er) benefits. That is, assuming you have reached full retirement age by the time you claim surviving divorced spouse benefits:

- If your ex-spouse died prior to full retirement age without having filed for retirement benefits, your widow(er) benefit will be 100% of your deceased ex-spouse's primary insurance amount.
- If your ex-spouse died after reaching full retirement age without having filed for retirement benefits, your widow(er) benefit will be equal to the amount your deceased ex-spouse would have received if he/she had filed on the date of death.
- If your ex-spouse was already claiming benefits by the time of death, your widow(er) benefit will be equal to the greater of the amount your deceased ex-spouse was receiving prior to death, or 82.5% of your deceased ex-spouse's primary insurance amount.

If you claim surviving divorced spouse benefits prior to FRA, the benefit you receive will be reduced.

And as with regular widow(er) benefits, if you claim surviving divorced spouse benefits at the same time that you're receiving a retirement benefit, the total amount you receive will be the greater of the two benefit amounts.[1]

If You've Remarried

If you remarry before age 60, you will usually not be eligible for benefits on your prior spouse's record, unless your new spouse dies or you get divorced (that is, divorced from your second spouse), in which case you will again be eligible for benefits on your first spouse's record. If your second marriage also lasted ten years, you can claim benefits on behalf of either ex-spouse.

EXAMPLE: Anne is married to Bob for 15 years. Then they get divorced, and Anne marries Christopher. After 15 years of marriage to Christopher, they too get divorced. When Anne reaches age 62, she can claim spousal benefits on behalf of either ex-spouse. Because Bob made more than Christopher over the course of his career, Anne chooses to claim spousal benefits on behalf of Bob.

A few years later, Christopher dies. Anne is now eligible for surviving divorced spouse benefits

---

[1] Again, technically, if the widow(er) benefit is greater than your own retirement benefit, you receive your own retirement benefit, plus the widow(er) benefit, after reducing the widow(er) benefit by the amount of your own retirement benefit.

on his behalf. Despite Christopher's lower earnings, surviving divorced spouse benefits on his behalf are greater than divorced spouse benefits on Bob's behalf (because divorced spouse benefits are based on 50% of the ex-spouse's benefit, whereas surviving divorced spouse benefits are based on 100% of the deceased ex-spouse's benefit). So Anne switches to claiming surviving divorced spouse benefits on Christopher's behalf.

A few years later, Bob dies too. Anne can now switch to receiving surviving divorced spouse benefits on Bob's behalf (which, because of Bob's higher earnings, should be greater than the surviving divorced spouse benefits on Christopher's behalf that Anne had been receiving).

Chapter 5 Simple Summary

- The eligibility requirements for divorced spouse benefits are very similar to the requirements for spousal benefits for still-married couples, with the notable exception that the marriage must have lasted at least 10 years. (Ditto for the eligibility requirements for surviving divorced spouse benefits.)

- For the most part, benefits based on the work record of an ex-spouse are calculated the same way as benefits based on the work record of a current spouse.

- If, after divorcing your first spouse, you marry somebody else prior to age 60, you will usually not be eligible for spousal benefits based on the work record of your first spouse.

CHAPTER SIX

Child Benefits

The children of people who are receiving retirement (or disability) benefits, as well as the children of people who have died, may be eligible for a Social Security benefit of their own. To be eligible for such benefits, a child must:

1. Be a dependent of the worker in question,[1]
2. Be the child, legally adopted child, or step-child of the worker,[2]
3. Be unmarried, and

---

[1] The definition of "dependent" in this context is not the same as the definition that's used for the purpose of determining whether you can claim somebody as a dependent on your tax return. See Code of Federal Regulations sections 404.360 through 404.365 for details: http://www.ssa.gov/OP_Home/cfr20/404/404-0000.htm

[2] Grandchildren and step-grandchildren can also qualify if the child's parents are deceased or disabled and the other requirements are met.

4. Be under age 18 or be disabled with a disability that began before age 22.

Calculating Children's Benefits

In the case of children qualifying for benefits based on the earnings record of a retired or disabled worker, the amount of the child's benefit is 50% of the worker's primary insurance amount. For children of deceased workers, the child's benefit is 75% of the deceased worker's primary insurance amount. In either case, however, the amount the child actually receives could be reduced as a result of the family maximum.

Family Maximum

There is a maximum amount that a family can receive based on the work record of a given person. That maximum ranges from 150% to 187% of the person's primary insurance amount. For 2012, the maximum is calculated as:

- 150% of the first $980 of the worker's PIA, plus
- 272% of the worker's PIA from $981 to $1,415, plus
- 134% of the worker's PIA from $1,416 to $1,845, plus
- 175% of the worker's PIA over $1,845.

When the amount that a family would ordinarily receive (prior to considering the maximum) exceeds the maximum calculated based on that person's PIA, the benefits of each person other than the worker are reduced proportionately to keep the total amount the family receives under the maximum.

EXAMPLE: John and Claire are married, both at their full retirement age, with two dependent legally adopted children under the age of 18. John's primary insurance amount is $1,800, meaning that the family maximum benefit based on his work record (calculated using the rules on the previous page) is $3,169. Claire's work history is not sufficient for her to receive a retirement benefit of her own.

If John claims his own benefit exactly at his full retirement age, and Claire claims her spousal benefit exactly at full retirement age, the members of John's family would be eligible for the following benefits (prior to considering the family maximum):

- John: $1,800
- Claire: $900
- Child 1: $900
- Child 2: $900

The total of those four benefits is $4,500, which is well beyond the $3,169 family maximum based on John's work record. As a result, the benefits received by Claire and each of the two children will be reduced proportionately until the family's total benefit is under the maximum. (In the end, John will receive his $1,800, and the other three will each receive $456.)

It's important to note that the formula uses the worker's primary insurance amount rather than the monthly benefit he/she is actually receiving. So even if John had claimed his retirement benefit earlier or later than full retirement age, such that he was receiving an amount smaller or larger than his primary insurance amount, the amounts that Claire and the children receive would not change.

Also of note: If Claire was *not* receiving a spousal benefit, and was instead receiving a retirement benefit based on her own work record, her benefit would not count toward the family maximum. (As mentioned above, the family maximum is only the maximum that can be received with regard to one particular worker's work record.) As a result, each of the two children would be able to receive a larger benefit.

Important note: Benefits as a divorced spouse or surviving divorced spouse will not be reduced due to the family maximum. Nor, in turn, will the benefits of an ex-spouse be counted toward the maximum benefit for the rest of the family.

Effect of Children on Spousal Benefits

In addition to potentially qualifying for benefits themselves, children can often cause a parent to be eligible for benefits when they would not otherwise be eligible. Specifically, if you meet all of the requirements to collect spousal benefits aside from the fact that you are not yet 62 years old, you can still qualify for benefits if you have in your care a child who is under 16 or disabled and who is entitled to child's benefits on your spouse's work record.

Chapter 6 Simple Summary

- If they are under age 18 or disabled, children of people receiving retirement or disability benefits may be eligible for a benefit of up to 50% of the worker's primary insurance amount.

- If they are under age 18 or disabled, children of people who have died may be eligible for a benefit of up to 75% of the deceased parent's primary insurance amount.

- There is a maximum benefit that can be paid to a family (not including divorced spouses) based on the work record of a single person. That benefit can range from 150% to 187% of the worker's primary insurance amount.

- In the event that a family would exceed the maximum benefit, the benefits of each person other than the worker will be reduced proportionately until the total amount the family receives is below the maximum.

CHAPTER SEVEN

Social Security with a Pension

If you receive a pension from a job for which you did not have to pay Social Security taxes (e.g. work as an employee of a local government), any Social Security benefits you would otherwise be eligible to receive could be reduced by two special rules:

1. The Windfall Elimination Provision (WEP), or
2. The Government Pension Offset (GPO).

Note that neither of these rules applies in the case of a worker who receives a pension from work that was subject to Social Security taxes.

Windfall Elimination Provision

If you receive a pension from a job for which you did not have to pay Social Security taxes, the Windfall Elimination Provision (WEP) will result in you receiving a smaller Social Security benefit for any other work that you did—that is, work that *was* covered by Social Security taxes.

EXAMPLE: Elena works for 21 years as a police officer—a job in which she does not pay Social Security taxes. She then works for another 19 years for a private security firm. Because of her work for the local government, Elena qualifies for a pension. And because of her work for the security firm, she also qualifies for Social Security. The Windfall Elimination Provision will reduce the amount of Social Security benefits that Elena receives.

The Windfall Elimination Provision works by changing the formula used to calculate your primary insurance amount.[1] From there, any percentage adjustments are applied as normal for claiming earlier or later than full retirement age.

As discussed in Chapter 2, for people not affected by the WEP, Social Security replaces a certain percentage of their average monthly earnings from their 35 highest-earning years, after adjusting those

---

[1] Because it changes your primary insurance amount, the WEP also has an effect on the amount(s) your spouse or children can receive based on your work record.

earnings for wage inflation. For somebody becoming eligible for Social Security in 2012, if claimed at full retirement age, Social Security would replace:

- 90% of average indexed monthly earnings (AIME) up to $767, plus
- 32% of AIME from $767 to $4,624, plus
- 15% of AIME beyond $4,624.[1]

The Windfall Elimination Provision changes that 90% number (in the first line of the calculation) to a lower number, depending on the number of years in which you had "substantial earnings" covered by Social Security taxes. (The threshold for "substantial earnings" changes by year. For 2012, it is $20,475.)

- If you have 20 or fewer years with substantial earnings, the figure used will be 40% instead of 90%.
- For each year of substantial earnings beyond 20, the figure increases by 5% (until you reach the original 90% figure).

Important exception: The Windfall Elimination Provision will never reduce a worker's primary insurance amount by more than 50% of the worker's monthly pension amount. (If you are paid a pension in the form of a lump sum, the pension will be recalculated as if it were paid monthly.)

---

[1] Note that earnings from work not subject to Social Security tax would not be included in this calculation.

Government Pension Offset

If you receive a pension from work you did for a federal, state, or local government agency, and you did not have to pay Social Security taxes on your earnings from that work, the Government Pension Offset (GPO) reduces any Social Security spousal or survivor benefits you would receive based on your spouse's work record. The reduction in monthly benefits is calculated as $^2/_3$ of the monthly pension amount you receive. (Again, in the case of a pension taken as a lump sum, the reduction will be calculated as if the pension had been paid out on a monthly basis.)

EXAMPLE: Bob worked for many years in an administrative role for his local fire department. Bob's job was not subject to Social Security taxes. Upon his retirement at age 67, Bob gets a monthly pension of $2,100 per month. At her full retirement age, Bob's wife Janice begins claiming her Social Security benefit of $2,000 per month.

Ordinarily, this would mean that Bob could get a spousal Social Security benefit of $1,000 per month (50% of Janice's $2,000) as long as he claims it at full retirement age or later. However, because of the Government Pension Offset, Bob's monthly spousal benefit will be reduced by $1,400 ($^2/_3$ of his $2,100 monthly pension), thereby eliminating it completely.

Upon Janice's death, Bob will be able to claim a Social Security survivor benefit on Janice's record.

Ordinarily, since Janice claimed her benefit at her full retirement age and because Bob is claiming the survivor benefit after full retirement age, he'd be able to get the $2,000 per month that she was receiving. But, again, the GPO will reduce the benefit by $1,400, thereby leaving him with a monthly survivor benefit of $600.

Chapter 7 Simple Summary

- If you receive a pension from work you did that was not covered by Social Security taxes, the Windfall Elimination Provision (WEP) will reduce the Social Security benefits you (and your spouse or children, if applicable) can receive from any work you did that *was* covered by Social Security taxes.

- The degree to which your retirement benefit is reduced by the WEP depends on how many years you had "substantial earnings" that were covered by Social Security taxes.

- If you receive a pension from government work you did that was not covered by Social Security taxes, the Government Pension Offset will reduce any spousal or widow(er) Social Security benefits you could receive by $2/3$ of the amount of your pension.

CHAPTER EIGHT

The Earnings Test

If your retirement plan includes a stage of semi-retirement, you'll want to take the Social Security earnings test into consideration when making your plans.

In brief, the earnings test says that, for years before full retirement age during which you work while claiming your own retirement benefit, for every $2 by which your annual earnings exceed a certain amount ($14,640 in 2012), your Social Security benefit for that year will be reduced by $1.

EXAMPLE: Neal is two years away from full retirement age and is already claiming Social Security benefits. He worked this year and earned $25,000 (or $10,360 in excess of $14,640). As a result of the earnings test, his annual benefit will be reduced by $5,180 (half of the $10,360 excess).

There are four additional points worth noting here.

First, due to the "grace year" rule, which we'll discuss later in this chapter, it's likely that the earnings test will not reduce the amount you receive in your first year of retirement, even if you earn more than the annual threshold amount.

Second, after reaching full retirement age, the earnings test doesn't apply. You can earn as much as you want without a reduction in your benefits.

Third, for earnings test purposes, only wages, earnings from self-employment, and a few less-common types of income are considered. (For example, pension income, IRA distributions, interest income, and capital gains do *not* count.)[1]

Fourth, the calculation is different for the year in which you reach full retirement age. In that year:

- The exempt amount is higher ($38,880 for someone reaching FRA in 2012),
- $1 of benefits is withheld for every $3 of earnings in excess of the exempt amount rather than $1 being withheld for every $2 of excess earnings, and
- Earnings for months of the year after you reach FRA are not taken into consideration.

---

[1] For a full list of types of income that would be included for earnings test purposes, see Section 1811 of the Social Security Handbook:
http://www.ssa.gov/OP_Home/handbook/handbook.18/handbook-1811.html

How the Reduction Is Applied

Contrary to what you might expect, if your benefits are reduced as a result of the earnings test, they will not be reduced on a pro-rata basis throughout the year. Rather, your benefits will be withheld completely until the withholding requirement for the year has been satisfied.[1]

EXAMPLE: Aside from the earnings test, Laurie's Social Security benefit would be $18,000 per year ($1,500 per month). However, because of the test, her benefit will be reduced by $4,500 this year. As a result, Laurie will receive no benefits in January, February, or March. Then she will receive full benefits for the remaining nine months of the year.

When Laurie reaches full retirement age, her benefits will be recalculated to adjust for the months in which she didn't actually receive full benefits. That is, if she had claimed benefits 48 months before FRA, but the earnings test eliminated her benefits

---

[1] When you initially claim Social Security benefits, the SSA employee with whom you speak should ask you to estimate your annual earnings for that year as well as for the next year. This information will be used to determine how much of your benefits to withhold. If at any point during the year it becomes clear that you will earn significantly more or less than you had estimated, you can call the SSA to let them know to adjust your withholdings accordingly. At the end of each year, you will "settle up" with the SSA based on your actual earnings.

for 12 of those 48 months, her benefit will be recalculated as if she had only claimed 36 months early rather than 48.

Earnings Test for Spousal and Child Benefits

In the event that other family members are entitled to benefits based on your work record (e.g., spousal benefits or child benefits), the earnings test will reduce their benefits as well as yours if your earnings exceed the applicable threshold.

EXAMPLE: Prior to considering the earnings test, Winston is entitled to a retirement benefit of $1,000 per month, and his wife Donna is entitled to a spousal benefit of $500 per month. However, Winston is younger than full retirement age, and his annual earnings for the year are $29,000. As a result, the earnings test will reduce the family's total benefit for the year by $7,180 (half of the excess of $29,000 over $14,640).

Winston and Donna's $1,500 total monthly benefit will therefore be withheld entirely during the months of January, February, March, and April (by which point their benefits will have been reduced by $6,000 of the necessary $7,180). For May, their total benefit will have to be reduced by $1,180. Because Winston's benefit makes up two-thirds of their total benefit, two-thirds of the $1,180 reduction ($787) will be taken from his $1,000 benefit for the month.

The remaining one-third ($393) will be taken from Donna's $500 monthly benefit.

In addition, if somebody *else* (e.g., your spouse) is working while receiving benefits based on your work record, the earnings test could reduce that person's benefits (but not your own).

EXAMPLE: Prior to considering the earnings test, Winston is entitled to a retirement benefit of $1,000 per month, and his wife Donna is entitled to a spousal benefit of $500 per month.

However, Donna is younger than full retirement age, and her annual earnings for the year are $29,000. (This time we're assuming that Winston is completely retired.) In this case, the earnings test will reduce *Donna's* benefit for the year by $7,180 (half of the excess of $29,000 over $14,640). Winston's retirement benefit will not be affected. Because Donna's benefit prior to considering the earnings test is only $6,000 per year ($500 x 12), it will be eliminated completely for this year.

Earnings Test during First Year of Retirement

If you retire in the middle of the year, it's possible that the earnings test will not affect your benefits for the remainder of the year, even if by the date of your retirement you have already earned an amount greater than the annual threshold.

In Social Security jargon, the earnings test will not result in reduced benefits for any "non-service month in a grace year." A "non-service month" is a month in which you earn less than 1/12th of the annual threshold for the earnings test (so, $1,220 for 2012) or in which you do not perform substantial services for your business if you are self-employed.[1] And the first year in which you have a non-service month while claiming a retirement benefit, spousal benefit, or widow(er) benefit is called your "grace year."

EXAMPLE: Beverly retired on October 1, after earning $80,000 in the first nine months of the year. She claims her retirement benefit immediately, and she does not work at all for the remainder of the year.

Because Beverly is not working October through December, each of those months will be considered "non-service months." And because this is the first year in which she has a non-service month in which she is also claiming a retirement benefit, this year will be considered her "grace year." Therefore, despite the fact that Beverly earned well above the annual threshold amount for the earnings test, the earnings test will not reduce the benefits she

---

[1] Performing "substantial services" for your business usually means working more than 45 hours over the course of the month. It is possible, however, that working as few as 15 hours can be considered substantial services if you manage a large business or you work in a highly skilled occupation.

receives in October, November, or December, because each of those months is considered a non-service month in a grace year.

Chapter 8 Simple Summary

- Prior to full retirement age, if you work while collecting retirement benefits, the total amount your family receives based on your work record will be reduced by 50% of the amount by which your annual earnings exceed a certain threshold ($14,640 for 2012).

- If a family member is working while receiving a benefit based on your work record, their benefit (but not your own benefit) will be reduced if their earnings exceed the same threshold mentioned above.

- The earnings test does not apply after you reach full retirement age. And in the year in which you reach full retirement age, the reduction in benefits is smaller for a given level of earnings than it would be in prior years.

- Once you reach full retirement age, your benefit will be recalculated to account for months in which you did not receive benefits as a result of the earnings test.

PART THREE

Social Security Planning: When to Claim Benefits

CHAPTER NINE

When to Claim Benefits: Unmarried Retirees

Even if you are married, the place to start when trying to figure out when to claim Social Security is with a solid understanding of the (less complicated) analysis for unmarried retirees.

And before we go any further, let's make sure we're on the same page about an important point: The decision of when to retire is separate from the decision of when to claim Social Security benefits. For example, depending on circumstances, you might find that it makes sense to retire at a given age, yet hold off on claiming Social Security until a later date—maybe even several years later.

As we've discussed, the earlier you claim Social Security, the less you'll receive per month. For example, the following table (reproduced from Chapter 2) shows how retirement benefits are affected by the age at which you first claim them:

Age when you claim retirement benefits	Amount of retirement benefit
5 years before FRA	70% of PIA
4 years before FRA	75% of PIA
3 years before FRA	80% of PIA
2 years before FRA	86.67% of PIA
1 year before FRA	93.33% of PIA
at FRA	100% of PIA
1 year after FRA	108% of PIA
2 years after FRA	116% of PIA
3 years after FRA	124% of PIA
4 years after FRA	132% of PIA

In other words, by waiting until age 70 rather than claiming as early as possible at age 62, you can increase your monthly benefit amount by roughly three-quarters. Of course, by waiting, you decrease the *number* of months in which you'll be receiving a Social Security check.

So how can you tell if the trade-off is worth it? One way to compare two possible ages for claiming benefits is to compute the age to which you would have to live for one strategy to become superior to the other strategy. Another way to analyze the decision is to compare the payout you get from delaying Social Security to the level of income you can safely get from other retirement income sources.

Computing the Breakeven Point

EXAMPLE: Alex and Bob are both retired and unmarried. Both are age 62, both have a full retirement age of 66, and both have exactly the same earnings history. In fact, the only difference between the two is that Alex decides to claim his retirement benefit at age 62, while Bob decides to wait all the way until 70. Even though Alex claims benefits at age 62, he doesn't need to spend the money right now, so he keeps it in his savings account, where it earns a return that precisely matches inflation.

By age 70, because he has been receiving benefits for eight years, Alex is far better off than Bob. However, starting at age 70, Bob starts to catch up (because he's receiving a monthly benefit equal to 132% of his primary insurance amount, as compared to Alex who is receiving a monthly benefit equal to 75% of his primary insurance amount).

In the end, Bob's cumulative benefit surpasses Alex's cumulative benefit approximately half way through age 80. From age 80.5 onward, Bob's lead over Alex continues to grow.

The takeaway: For an unmarried retiree, from a breakeven perspective, if you live past age 80.5, you will have been better off claiming benefits at age 70 instead of claiming as early as possible at age 62.[1]

---

[1] While our example above assumed a full retirement age of 66, the breakeven point for people with an FRA of 67 is not meaningfully different. (Specifically, it occurs a little less than two months earlier.)

According to the Social Security Administration, the average total life expectancy for a 62-year-old female is 84.3. For a male, it's 81.4.[1] In other words, from a breakeven perspective, most unmarried retirees will be best served by delaying benefits as long as possible.

Comparing Social Security to Other Income Options

When you delay Social Security, you give up a certain amount of money right now (i.e., this month's or this year's benefits) in exchange for a stream of payments that will increase with inflation for the rest of your life.

Take, for example, somebody born in 1950 (who would have a full retirement age of 66). If her benefit at full retirement age would be $1,000 per month, her benefit at age 62 would be $750 per month, and at age 63 it would be $800 per month.

Therefore, waiting from age 62 to age 63 is the equivalent of paying $9,000 (that is, $750 forgone per month, for 12 months) in exchange for a source of income that pays $600 per year (that is, a $50 increase in monthly retirement benefit, times 12 months per year), adjusted for inflation, for the rest of her life.

---

[1] From the life expectancy table available at:
http://www.ssa.gov/oact/STATS/table4c6.html

Dividing $600 by $9,000 shows us that delaying Social Security retirement benefits from age 62 to 63 provides a 6.67% payout. Let's see how that compares to other sources of retirement income.

Inflation-adjusted single premium immediate lifetime annuities are essentially pensions that you can purchase from an insurance company. With such an annuity, you pay the insurance company an initial lump-sum (the premium for the policy), and they promise to pay you a certain amount of income, adjusted for inflation, for the rest of your life. In other words, such annuities are a source of income *very* similar to Social Security.

As of this writing, according to the quote system on mutual fund company Vanguard's website (which allows you to compare quotes from multiple insurance companies), the highest payout available to a 63-year-old female on such an annuity is 3.95%. For a male, the highest available payout would be 4.42%.[1] As you can see, both of these figures fall well short of the 6.67% payout that comes from delaying Social Security from 62 to 63.

Alternatively, we can compare the payout from delaying Social Security to the income that you can safely draw from a typical portfolio of stocks and bonds. Several studies have shown that, historically in the U.S., retirees trying to fund a 30-year retirement run a significant risk of running out of money

---

[1] You can access the quote system via the following page, but you will need a Vanguard account to do so: https://personal.vanguard.com/us/whatweoffer/annuities/income

when they use inflation-adjusted withdrawal rates greater than 4%.[1] And it's worth noting that even a 4% withdrawal rate isn't a sure bet going forward, given that the studies show 4% to be *mostly* safe in the *past*, which is a far cry from *completely* safe in the *future*.

In other words, for each dollar of Social Security you give up now (by delaying benefits), you can expect to receive a greater level of income in the future than you could safely take from a dollar invested in a typical stock/bond portfolio.

A similar analysis can be performed for each year up to age 70, and the conclusion is the same: Delaying Social Security benefits can be an excellent way to increase the amount of income you can safely take from your portfolio.

EXAMPLE: Daniel is retired at 62 years old. His full retirement age is 66. He has $40,000 of annual expenses and a $600,000 portfolio. He is trying to decide between claiming benefits as early as possible at age 62 or spending down his portfolio while he holds off on claiming benefits until age 70.

Daniel's primary insurance amount (the amount he'd receive per month if he claimed his

---

[1] The most famous such study is the so-called "Trinity Study" by three professors (Cooley, Hubbard, and Walz) at Trinity University. The actual title of the study was "Retirement Savings: Choosing a Withdrawal Rate That Is Sustainable," and you can find it online at:
http://www.aaii.com/journal/article/retirement-savings-choosing-a-withdrawal-rate-that-is-sustainable

retirement benefit at full retirement age) is $1,500, which means he would receive:

- $1,125 per month ($13,500 per year) if he claimed benefits at age 62, or
- $1,980 per month ($23,760 per year) if he claimed benefits at age 70.

If Daniel claims his retirement benefit at age 62, he'll have to satisfy $26,500 of expenses every year from his portfolio (because Social Security will only be satisfying $13,500 out of $40,000). That is, he'll be using a 4.4% withdrawal rate ($26,500 divided by his $600,000 portfolio) starting at age 62. That's a higher withdrawal rate than most experts would recommend.

Alternatively, if Daniel delays Social Security until 70, he'll have to satisfy annual expenses of $16,240 (that is, $40,000, minus $23,760 in Social Security benefits), plus an additional $23,760 for the eight years until he claims Social Security.

If Daniel allocates $190,080 (that is, $23,760 x 8) of his $600,000 portfolio to cash or something else very low-risk (in order to satisfy the additional expenses for those eight years), that leaves him with a typical stock/bond portfolio of $409,920. With a portfolio of $409,920, Daniel can satisfy his remaining $16,240 of annual expenses using a withdrawal rate of just under 4%.

In effect, Daniel is spending down his portfolio by $190,080 in order to purchase additional Social Security benefits in the amount of $10,260 per year, starting at age 70. By doing so, he's reduced the withdrawal rate that he'll need to use from his portfolio for the remainder of his life, thereby reducing the probability that he'll run out of money. In addition, if Daniel's portfolio performs very poorly and he *does* run out of money, he'll be much better off in the wait-until-70 scenario than in the claim-at-62 scenario, because he'll be left with $23,760 of Social Security per year rather than $13,500.

Reasons Not to Delay Social Security

Of course, there are circumstances in which it would *not* make sense for an unmarried investor to delay taking Social Security.

First and most obviously, if your finances are such that you absolutely *need* the income right now, then you have little choice in the matter.

Second, if you have reason to think that your life expectancy is well below average, it may be advantageous to claim benefits early. For example, if you have a medical condition such that you don't expect to make it past age 64, it would obviously not make a great deal of sense to choose to wait until age 70 to claim benefits.

Third, the higher market interest rates are, the less attractive it is to delay Social Security. For example, if inflation-adjusted interest rates (such as those on inflation-protected Treasury bonds known as TIPS) were approximately 3% higher than they are right now, the payout from inflation-adjusted lifetime annuities might be *higher* than the payout from delaying Social Security.

Chapter 9 Simple Summary

- For unmarried retirees, from a breakeven perspective, you'll be best served by holding off on benefits all the way until age 70 if you expect to live past age 80.5. (And, for reference, the average total life expectancy for a 62-year-old female is 84.3. For a male, it's 81.4.)

- For unmarried retirees, on a dollar-for-dollar basis, the lifetime income you gain from delaying Social Security is generally greater than the level of income you can safely get from other sources. As a result, delaying Social Security can be a great way to increase the amount you can safely spend per year. (Or, said differently, it can be a great way to reduce the likelihood that you will outlive your money.)

- The shorter your life expectancy and the greater the available yield on inflation-protected bonds, the less desirable it becomes to delay claiming Social Security benefits.

CHAPTER TEN

When to Claim Benefits:
Married Couples with One Working Spouse

In keeping with the plan of adding complexity one layer at a time, let's move on to the next-simplest Social Security retirement scenario: a married couple, only one of whom worked long enough to be eligible for his/her own retirement benefit.

When Should the Working Spouse Claim Benefits?

As we discussed in the previous chapter, delaying Social Security is akin to buying an inflation-adjusted lifetime annuity—one that's a heck of a deal for many investors because it comes with a significantly higher payout and lower credit risk than annuities you can buy in the private marketplace.

For the working spouse in our scenario, delaying Social Security is just like that, but better. In addition to an unusually high payout and unusually low credit risk, the annuity now comes with the possibility of a survivor benefit as well.

EXAMPLE: Allan and Liz are married, both age 62. Because Liz spent many years out of the paid workforce doing volunteer work and raising their children, she did not earn enough Social Security credits to be eligible for a retirement benefit of her own.

After either Allan or Liz dies, the surviving spouse will be receiving an amount equal to Allan's benefit. (If Liz is the surviving spouse, it will be in the form of a widow's benefit.) As a result, if Allan chooses to hold off on claiming his own retirement benefit, he increases not only his own benefit while he's alive, but also Liz's widow's benefit in the event that he predeceases her.

In short, the decision for the working spouse includes the same considerations as for an unmarried retiree, with one major modification: The life expectancy in question is no longer just the person's own life expectancy, but rather the combined life expectancy of the two spouses (because delaying benefits will increase the amount paid out as long as *either* spouse is alive).

In other words, from a breakeven perspective, for it to be advantageous for the working spouse to delay his/her benefit all the way until 70, only *one* spouse needs to make it to the point at which the working spouse would have reached age 80.5. As you can imagine, this often means that it's a very good deal for the working spouse to hold off on claiming benefits until age 70.

It's worth noting that the age difference between the spouses becomes an important factor here. For example, if Liz from our example above was 10 years younger than Allan rather than his same age, it would be *especially* advantageous for Allan to delay taking benefits, because it would now be exceedingly likely that one spouse will make it to the point at which Allan would be age 80.5 (because Liz would only have to live to age 70.5 for that to be true). In contrast, if Liz was 10 years *older* than Allan, it would be relatively *less* advantageous for Allan to delay taking benefits—though it would still be more advantageous than it is for an unmarried person to do so, because there's at least some possibility that Liz will outlive Allan.

When Should the Other Spouse Claim Benefits?

For the non-working spouse, the decision of when to claim spousal benefits works in much the same way as the decision for an unmarried person trying to decide when to claim retirement benefits, but with two modifications:

1. There is no benefit to waiting beyond full retirement age to claim spousal benefits, as they do not continue to increase for waiting beyond that point, and
2. It's somewhat *less* advantageous for the nonworking spouse to delay benefits, because doing so only increases the amount the couple will receive while they're *both* alive.

For example, if we look back at Allan and Liz from above, having Liz hold off on claiming Social Security does not increase the amount Allan will receive at any point. And it only increases the amount Liz will receive while Allan is still alive as well (because once Allan dies, Liz will switch to her widow's benefit).

For the nonworking spouse trying to decide between claiming at age 62 or waiting until full retirement age (assuming his/her full retirement age is 66), the breakeven point would be about one third of the way through age 74. In this case, however, *both* spouses would still need to be alive by the time the nonworking spouse reaches age 74 for it to be advantageous to delay all the way to full retirement age.

Chapter 10 Simple Summary

- For married couples, *both* spouses' respective life expectancies should be considered in *each* spouse's claiming decision.

- For married couples in which only one spouse is eligible for a Social Security retirement benefit, it is often particularly advantageous to have that spouse delay claiming his/her benefit as long as possible, because doing so increases the amount the couple will receive as long as either spouse is alive.

- From a breakeven perspective, it makes sense for the working spouse to wait until 70 if *either* spouse is expected to live until the point at which the working spouse would be age 80.5.

- For the spouse who is not eligible for his/her own retirement benefit, there's less to be gained as a result of waiting until full retirement age to claim spousal benefits, because doing so only increases the amount the couple will receive while they're both alive. (And there's nothing to be gained for waiting *beyond* full retirement age, because spousal benefits do not continue to increase as a result of waiting past FRA.)

CHAPTER ELEVEN

When to Claim Benefits: Married Couples with Two Working Spouses

Now we get to the most complex scenario: two spouses, each of whom is eligible for a retirement benefit of his/her own. At a basic level, the decision is analogous to the decision for married couples with only one person who can claim a retirement benefit. That is:

- The couple stands to gain the most from having the higher-earning spouse delay his/her benefits as long as possible, and
- The couple stands to gain less from having the lower-earning spouse delay benefits.

In addition to the above considerations, however, there are some clever strategies available to married couples that (depending on circumstances) might allow them to maximize their Social Security benefits even further.

The "Restricted Application" Strategy

As we've discussed previously, after reaching full retirement age, if you're eligible for both spousal benefits and your own retirement benefit, you can file for one or the other. (This is in contrast to filing for one or the other prior to full retirement age, in which case you would automatically be deemed to have filed for the other benefit as well.)

EXAMPLE: Steve and Beth are both age 60, and they each have a full retirement age of 66. Beth's earnings history is slightly higher than Steve's, so they decide to have Beth delay her retirement benefit until age 70. However, to help with their near-term cash flow, they choose to have Steve take his benefits at age 62.

When Beth reaches full retirement age, she can file a "restricted application" for just her spousal benefit. Four years later, when Beth reaches age 70, she files for her own retirement benefit.

Result: Beth receives spousal benefits for four years (from age 66 to 70) at essentially no cost to her, since her own retirement benefit is growing the entire time because she had not yet filed for it. Depending on the size of Steve's primary insurance amount, these four years of spousal benefits could be a large five-figure sum—which Beth and Steve would miss out on entirely if they were less familiar with the Social Security rules.

The "File and Suspend" Strategy

Alternatively, if you are full retirement age, you can apply for your own retirement benefit, then ask to have payments suspended. This satisfies the requirement that you must have claimed your own benefit in order for your spouse to receive a spouse's benefit, but because you are not actually *receiving* your own retirement benefit, your benefit continues to grow until age 70.

EXAMPLE: Katie and Joe are married. They are both age 62, and they both have a full retirement age of 66. Joe has earned substantially more than Katie over the course of their careers—so much more, in fact, that Katie's spousal benefit is going to be almost twice the size of her own retirement benefit.

Like Steve and Beth above, Katie and Joe decide to have the higher earner wait until 70 and the lower earner claim as early as possible at age 62. So far, you'll notice that this is the same as the "restricted application" strategy outlined above. At full retirement age, however, the strategies diverge.

Once Joe reaches full retirement age, instead of filing a restricted application for just spousal benefits, he files for his *own* benefit and asks to have payments immediately suspended. This allows Katie to switch to her (larger) spousal benefit, and it allows Joe's own retirement benefit (and Katie's survivor benefit, if she should outlive him) to continue growing until Joe reaches age 70.

In general, the file and suspend strategy (as outlined above) will be preferable to the restricted application strategy outlined above any time the higher-earning spouse has a primary insurance amount that's at least two-and-a-half times the size of the lower-earning spouse's primary insurance amount.

Combining Both Strategies

If both spouses want to delay their own retirement benefit until age 70, it may be possible to combine the two strategies above in order to get 3-4 years of drawback-free spousal benefits for one spouse.

EXAMPLE: Christopher and Patricia are married, and they both reached their full retirement age of 66 this year. They have similar earnings histories, and they both want to delay their retirement benefits until age 70.

Upon reaching full retirement age, Patricia files for benefits and asks to have payments immediately suspended. Christopher (who has also reached full retirement age) then files a restricted application for spousal benefits only (as outlined in the first strategy above). Then, at age 70, Christopher switches to his own retirement benefit, and Patricia ends the suspension of her benefit payments.

Result: Christopher is able to receive spousal benefits for four years (from age 66 to 70), while they both allow their own retirement benefits to grow until age 70.

Chapter 11 Simple Summary

- It's often a good idea to have the spouse with the higher primary insurance amount delay taking benefits, because doing so increases the amount the couple receives as long as either spouse is alive.

- It's less advantageous to have the spouse with the lower primary insurance amount delay benefits, because doing so only increases the amount the couple will receive while they're both alive. That said, depending on circumstances, it can still be a good idea for the lower earner to delay benefits.

- With clever planning, it's often possible to have one spouse receive spousal benefits for the years between full retirement age and age 70, while allowing the higher-earning spouse's own retirement benefit to continue growing until age 70.

CHAPTER TWELVE

Taking Social Security Early to Invest It

In our discussions up to this point, when determining the breakeven point for delaying benefits, we've assumed a 0% inflation-adjusted return for the money. That is, we've assumed that when people take benefits early, that money sits around someplace where it keeps up with, but does not outpace, inflation. (Alternatively, we're assuming that they're spending their Social Security benefits—and therefore spending less from their portfolio per year—and that the additional money left in their portfolio keeps up with but does not outpace inflation.)

Given current interest rates (with yields on inflation-protected Treasury bonds negative all the way up to 10-year maturities), that happens to be a fairly reasonable assumption. However, inflation-adjusted interest rates are not always at or near zero. In addition, some retirees may be happy to take some risk with their money in the hope of earning higher returns.

As we've discussed previously, for an unmarried retiree with a full retirement age of 66 who is trying to choose between claiming benefits at age 62, or holding off all the way until 70, the breakeven point (assuming a 0% inflation-adjusted return) comes approximately at age 80.5. That is, if the retiree dies before age 80.5, he/she will have been better off taking benefits early at 62. If the retiree lives past age 80.5, he/she will have been better off taking benefits at age 70.

So how does that breakeven point change when we assume an inflation-adjusted ("real") return greater than 0%?

Claiming at 62 vs. Claiming at 70 (assuming FRA of 66)	
Inflation-Adjusted Return	Breakeven Age (rounded to nearest year)
0%	81
1%	82
2%	83
3%	85
4%	87
5%	90

As you can see, the higher the after-inflation return you earn on your money, the more advantageous it becomes to take benefits early. That's because the head start you get with the "claim at 62" strategy is larger when you're earning a higher return on the benefits you receive from ages 62 to 70. And, naturally, the larger the head start, the longer it takes for the "claim at 70" strategy to close the gap.

Note that the breakeven points in the table above are also the breakeven points for the higher earner in a married couple, though rather than the higher earner needing to make it to the age in question, only one spouse needs to make it to the point at which the higher earner would have been the age in question.[1]

Of particular note here is the line showing the breakeven point for a 2% inflation-adjusted return. With a 2% real return, the break-even point occurs shortly before turning 83. As we mentioned earlier, according to the Social Security Administration, the total life expectancy at age 62 is 81.2 for a male and 84.1 for a female. In other words, at a 2% real return, the break-even point is approximately the same as the average life expectancy, meaning that, on average, an unmarried person (who only has to consider one life expectancy) would be approximately as well-off claiming at age 62 as at age 70.

---

[1] The breakeven points for the spouse with the lower earnings history are more complicated because they vary depending on whether we're talking about a spousal benefit or a retirement benefit.

What If We Use Riskier Investments?

If we assume, for example, a 5% after-inflation return, the break-even point occurs around age 90. In other words, with a 5% real return, most retirees would end up benefiting from claiming benefits early and investing them.

And indeed, a 5% after-inflation return does sound reasonable for a low-cost diversified stock portfolio. But it's far from a slam-dunk. For example, of the sixty-seven 20-year periods from 1926-2011, nineteen of them had real returns below 5%.[1]

As it turns out, the conclusion here is rather common sense: If you take something with very little risk (that is, your Social Security payments) and you replace it with high-risk investments (e.g., stocks), there's a decent chance you'll end up with more money. But that comes at a very real cost (specifically, a higher risk of running out of money if things go poorly).

---

[1] According to the data for large company U.S. stocks from Morningstar's *Ibbotson SBBI 2012 Classic Yearbook*.

Chapter 12 Simple Summary

- The higher the inflation-adjusted rate of return you can earn on your money, the more advantageous it becomes to claim benefits early and invest the money (because the higher rate of return means that it takes longer for the "claim at 70" strategy to catch up to strategies where you claim benefits earlier).

- Delaying Social Security retirement benefits until 70 is a great way to reduce the risk of running out of money during your lifetime. It also, however, reduces the likelihood of a very-high-return scenario that could potentially occur if you take the money early and invest it.

PART FOUR

Other Related Retirement-Planning Topics

CHAPTER THIRTEEN

Checking Your Earnings Record

The Social Security Administration used to send a statement each year that included your earnings record by year, as well as an estimate of what your Social Security retirement benefit would be if you claimed it at age 62, at full retirement age, or at age 70.

Then, in 2011, the SSA stopped sending those statements in an attempt to save on costs. Near the beginning of 2012, however, the SSA announced that they now offer an online version of the statement at SSA.gov/mystatement (after you jump through some hoops to verify your identity, that is).

In addition, the SSA also announced that annual paper statements have been resumed for people age 60 or over who are not already receiving benefits, and that a single paper statement will be sent to people in the year they turn 25.

Checking Your Earnings Record

In addition to being helpful for the purpose of getting an estimate of your Social Security retirement benefits, creating an account on the Social Security website is helpful because it allows you to check your earnings record. Mistakes happen, and it's best to get them fixed as quickly as possible.

However, according to the SSA, if your record is missing earnings from this year or last year, it's not necessarily a problem. Most likely, it simply means that the earnings haven't been recorded just yet. They should appear on a later statement.

Correcting Mistakes in Your Earnings Record

If you find that your earnings record is missing earnings (other than those from this year or last year), you'll want to find something that documents the correct amount of earnings, for example:

- Your Form 1040 from the year in question,
- Applicable Forms W-2,
- Applicable pay stubs, or
- If you were self-employed, Schedule C or Schedule SE from that year.

Once you've found something documenting your earnings, you'll want to call the SSA to get things straightened out as soon as possible.

Where to Find Earnings Documentation

If you no longer have anything documenting your earnings for the year in question, you could call your employer from that year to request your W-2 or, failing that, some other sort of payroll record.

Alternatively, you can order a transcript of that year's tax return from the IRS. A tax return transcript includes most information that was filed on your return for the year, including any accompanying schedules or forms. You can request a transcript in any of three ways:

1. Calling the IRS at 1-800-908-9946,
2. Ordering it online[1], or
3. Sending in Form 4506-T.

If you worked as an employee, the figure that should show up for a given year's earnings record on the Social Security website is the number from box 3 ("Social Security wages") from your Form W-2 for the year. If you had multiple jobs, it should be the

---

[1] You can do this at:
http://www.irs.gov/individuals/article/0,,id=232168,00.html

total of all your box 3's (limited to the maximum earnings subject to Social Security tax for the year). The reason they don't use box 1 is that the calculation for box 1 includes reductions for things like pre-tax 401(k) contributions, which reduce income taxes but not Social Security taxes.

If you were self-employed, the figure that should appear on your Social Security earnings record is line 4 ("net earnings from self-employment") from Schedule SE. Note that this amount is not the same as the profit from your business. Rather, it's 92.35% of the profit from your business, to account for the deduction you get for one-half of your self-employment tax.

Chapter 13 Simple Summary

- By creating an account on the Social Security website (at ssa.gov/mystatement), you can get an estimate of your retirement benefits and you can check your earnings record for errors.

- In the event that you do find an error in your earnings record, you'll want to send the SSA proof of your actual earnings from that year. If you don't have any such proof, and cannot get any from your employer, you can contact the IRS to get a transcript of the applicable tax return.

CHAPTER FOURTEEN

How Is Social Security Taxed?

Each year, the portion of your Social Security income that's subject to federal income tax depends on your "combined income." Your combined income is equal to:

- Your adjusted gross income (AGI), which you can find at the bottom of the first page of your Form 1040, plus
- Any tax-exempt interest you earned, plus
- 50% of your Social Security benefits.

If your combined income is below $25,000 ($32,000 if married filing jointly), none of your Social Security benefits will be taxed.

For every dollar of combined income above that level, $0.50 of benefits will become taxable until 50% of your benefits are taxed or until you reach

$34,000 of combined income ($44,000 if married filing jointly).

For every dollar of combined income above $34,000 ($44,000 if married filing jointly), $0.85 of Social Security benefits will become taxable—all the way up to the point at which 85% of your Social Security benefits are taxable.[1]

Important note: To say that 85% of your Social Security benefits are taxable does not mean that 85% of your benefits will disappear to taxes. Rather, it means that 85% of your benefits will be included as taxable income when determining your total income tax for the year.

How Does This Affect Tax/Retirement Planning?

The big takeaway of the above calculations is that, once you start collecting Social Security, your marginal tax rate (that is, the total tax rate you would pay on each additional dollar of income) often increases dramatically. That's because, if your "combined income" is in the applicable range, each additional dollar of income is not only taxed at your regular tax rate, it also causes an additional $0.50 or $0.85 of Social Security benefits to be taxable.

---

[1] These are the general rules. As with so many aspects of the tax code, there are exceptions. For more information, see IRS Publication 915, at:
http://www.irs.gov/pub/irs-pdf/p915.pdf

This dramatic change in your marginal tax rate often creates significant tax planning opportunities.

For example, if you haven't yet begun to collect Social Security and you realize that your marginal tax rate will increase once you do, you may benefit from funding most of your current spending via withdrawals from tax-deferred accounts (as opposed to taxable accounts or Roth accounts), thereby allowing the withdrawals to be taxed at your current, relatively-lower tax rate, and thereby preserving your Roth accounts for funding spending needs in the future when your tax rate will be higher.

Or you might even want to take it one step further by converting a portion of your traditional IRA(s) to a Roth IRA in the years of retirement prior to collecting Social Security.

Or, if you are already collecting Social Security, once your combined income nears the range where Social Security benefits will start to become taxable, you may want to fund the rest of your spending (to the extent possible) with assets *not* from tax-deferred accounts (so as to stay below the range where your benefits would become taxable).

Alternatively, if your combined income is already near the *high* end of the range in question (such that most or all of your benefits are 85% taxable), it may make sense to withdraw *more* from your tax-deferred accounts (perhaps just enough to put you up to the top of your current tax bracket) so that you can withdraw less next year, thereby allowing you to stay in the range where your benefits will not be taxable.

Chapter 14 Simple Summary

- Depending on how high your "combined income" is in a given year, your Social Security benefits could be nontaxable or partially taxable (with a maximum of 85% of them being included in your taxable income for the year).

- If it looks like your marginal tax rate is going to increase sharply once you start collecting Social Security, it may make sense—in the years prior to collecting Social Security—to fund much of your spending from tax-deferred accounts (and potentially execute Roth IRA conversions) to take advantage of the fact that your tax rate is lower than it will be in the future.

- Once you start collecting Social Security, you may be able to reduce your overall tax bill by carefully planning *which* accounts you spend from each year (tax-deferred as opposed to Roth as opposed to taxable) so as to minimize the portion of your Social Security benefits that will be taxable.

CHAPTER FIFTEEN

Social Security and Asset Allocation

Not only does your Social Security claiming strategy affect your tax planning, it has an impact on retirement portfolio considerations as well.

Planning to Wait to Claim Benefits?

Most advice about constructing and managing a retirement portfolio assumes that you'll be spending the same amount of money from your portfolio each year (after accounting for inflation). This assumption is decidedly unrealistic for anybody who doesn't intend to claim Social Security immediately upon retiring.

EXAMPLE: Roger is planning to retire at age 62. But because he has a family history of longevity, he's decided to wait until age 70 to claim his Social

Security retirement benefit. Roger expects his retirement spending needs to total approximately $40,000 per year. When Roger collects Social Security at age 70, his annual benefit will be $22,000. Roger has no sources of income other than his portfolio and his Social Security.

Rather than spending an equal amount from his portfolio each year, Roger will be spending $40,000 per year for eight years (from age 62 to 70). Then, from age 70 onward, he'll only be spending $18,000 per year ($40,000 minus his $22,000 annual benefit).

Roger might find it beneficial to mentally separate his assets into two distinct portfolios. One portfolio will be used to satisfy $22,000 of expenses per year for eight years (until his Social Security kicks in). The other portfolio will need to satisfy $18,000 of expenses every year, starting immediately upon retirement, for the remainder of Roger's life.

Because Roger's first portfolio will be entirely depleted within eight years, it should probably be invested in something very safe. Perhaps a low-risk bond fund would be a good choice, or maybe a CD ladder consisting of eight roughly equally-sized CDs (one maturing each year for eight years).

Roger's second portfolio will consist of the remainder of his financial assets. Because this portfolio is intended to satisfy an approximately steady level of spending ($18,000 per year), the conventional advice *would* apply. That is, Roger would probably benefit from constructing a diversified, low-cost portfolio (of low-cost index funds or

ETFs, for example) using an asset allocation that's suitable for his risk tolerance. Alternatively, if he is particularly risk-averse, Roger might find it beneficial to allocate a portion of this money to a lifetime inflation-adjusted annuity.

By mentally dividing his portfolio like this, Roger can easily see how much to put into very safe investments to satisfy his near-term spending needs for the years prior to collecting Social Security (in this case, approximately $176,000, or $22,000 for each of eight years) and how much to invest using a more long-term-oriented allocation.

For married couples, there is more complexity involved given that the two spouses will usually retire at different points in time and they will often claim Social Security at different points in time as well. But the general concept is the same: Make sure that you have enough safe assets to get you through to the point at which you'll start collecting Social Security. The remainder of the portfolio, which will be spent over a more extended period of time, can be invested more aggressively (though many retirees will still prefer to invest this part of the portfolio relatively conservatively).

Chapter 15 Simple Summary

- When deciding the asset allocation for your retirement portfolio, it can be helpful to think of it as two separate portfolios: One (invested very conservatively) that you will spend down in the years of retirement prior to collecting Social Security and one (invested more aggressively) that you will use for the remainder of your spending needs throughout your entire retirement.

CHAPTER SIXTEEN

Do-Over Options

If you've done much reading about Social Security, it's likely that you've encountered an article discussing the "do-over" strategy. Under this strategy, a person could claim benefits at age 62, then, at age 70, withdraw his/her application and repay all of the benefits received to date—with the result being that the SSA would recalculate the person's benefit as if he/she had never claimed prior to age 70. In effect, this allowed people to get a very large interest-free loan from the government.

To be as clear as possible: **This strategy is no longer an option.** In December of 2010, the Social Security Administration changed the rules to prevent people from doing this. (Unfortunately, many websites have old articles that they've never updated, which still show up prominently in online search results, making it likely that people will come across them.)

However, there still might be some things you can do to increase the amount of your monthly benefit if you've filed for Social Security benefits early and have since changed your mind.

12-Month Do-Over

The change in the rules didn't completely eliminate the ability to withdraw your application and pay back benefits received. Rather, it limited the do-over option in two ways:

1. It's now only available once per lifetime, and
2. It's now only available to people who have been receiving benefits for less than 12 months.

EXAMPLE: Beth files for benefits on her 64th birthday. Seven months later, she changes her mind and decides she'd rather wait until age 70. By filing Form SSA-521 and paying back all the benefits she's received so far, she can essentially undo her application, thereby allowing her Social Security benefit to grow until age 70.

It's worth noting, however, that the withdrawal of application process is not as easy as that one-page form makes it look, due to the facts that:

- Many SSA employees are not particularly familiar with the process, and

- There can be tax ramifications resulting from the repayment of benefits that you received in a prior year.[1]

Suspend Benefits at Full Retirement Age

If you've been receiving benefits for 12 months or more, it's not possible to pay back your benefits and start over. You can, however, suspend benefits once you reach full retirement age and choose not to start them again until a later date.

EXAMPLE: Greg's full retirement age is 66, and his primary insurance amount is $1,600. He begins claiming benefits at age 62, meaning that he receives $1,200 per month (that is, 75% of his PIA due to claiming four years early).

Three years later, he changes his mind and wishes he had waited. Once he reaches his full retirement age of 66, he can ask for his benefits to be suspended. If he waits until age 70 to start them again, he'll earn 4 years' worth of "delayed retirement credits," increasing his benefit by 8% for each year he waits, or 32% in total. Starting at age 70, Greg will receive $1,584 per month (calculated as his $1,600 PIA, times 75%, times 132%), which is close

---

[1] See IRS Publication 915 for more information: http://www.irs.gov/publications/p915/index.html

to the $1,600 per month he would have received if he'd originally started at full retirement age.

Social Security Earnings Test

Finally, if you claim benefits early and change your mind after missing the 12-month do-over window but before reaching your full retirement age, there's still one thing you can do that will help you offset the effect of claiming early: work.

As we discussed in Chapter 8, in years prior to full retirement age during which you work while claiming benefits, the Social Security earnings test will reduce your annual benefit by $1 for every $2 by which your annual earnings exceed a certain amount ($14,640 in 2012).

Then, after you reach full retirement age, your benefit will be recalculated to account for the benefits you didn't receive earlier. For example, if the earnings test reduced the total benefit you received by an amount equal to ten months of benefits, your benefit after full retirement age will be calculated as if you'd claimed ten months later than you actually did.[1]

---

[1] When recalculating your benefits at full retirement age, the SSA actually accounts for any month in which you didn't receive a full benefit. So if the earnings test eliminated your benefit for nine months, and cut it in half for a tenth month, your benefit at FRA would be recalculated as if you had missed out on ten months of benefits.

Backdating a Claim for Benefits

Alternatively, if you decide at some point that you wish you had claimed benefits *earlier* (whether retirement benefits, spousal benefits, widow(er) benefits or child benefits), you can request in your application that you receive benefits for up to six months prior to the month in which you actually file your application. Note, however, that you cannot receive benefits in this way for:

- A month in which you were not eligible for benefits, or
- A month prior to the month in which you reach your full retirement age. (This exception does not apply for child benefits.) [1]

For example, if you first file for retirement benefits in October of a given year and you decide that you should have filed for benefits earlier, you can effectively backdate your application to April (six months prior to October). If, however, you reached your full retirement age in July of that year, July would be the

---

[1] Under certain cases in which disability is involved, spousal benefits and widow(er) benefits may be retroactively obtained for up to *twelve* months prior to the date of application, and the full retirement age limit may not apply. See 404.621 of the Code of Federal Regulations for more information:
http://www.ssa.gov/OP_Home/cfr20/404/404-0621.htm

earliest month to which you could backdate your application.

Chapter 16 Simple Summary

- Unless you have been receiving benefits for less than 12 months, it's no longer possible to "undo" your application by filing a withdrawal of application form and paying back the benefits you've received to date.

- If, however, you claimed benefits early and changed your mind (and you're past the 12-month window), you can increase your future monthly benefit by working (thereby subjecting your benefits to the earnings test) prior to full retirement age, or by having payments suspended between full retirement age and age 70.

- When you first file for retirement, spousal, or widow(er) benefits, you can choose to backdate your application by up to six months (but no earlier than the month in which you reached full retirement age).

CONCLUSION

Six Social Security Rules of Thumb

Unfortunately, the Social Security rules can be bewilderingly complex. And to determine the very best claiming strategy for your family, you would have to understand how those rules interact with a whole list of variables, the most important of which—the age at which you (and your spouse if you're married) will die—is entirely unknowable.

Fortunately, there are six rules of thumb that can get you most of the way there.

RULE #1: The longer you expect to live (or the more worried you are about running out of money if you do live to have a long retirement), the better it is to hold off on taking benefits.

RULE #2: For an unmarried person trying to decide between claiming as early as possible at age 62 or as late as possible at age 70, the breakeven point is approximately age 80.5. That is, if the person lives beyond that point, he/she will have received more total benefits by waiting until 70 rather than claiming early. (And, for reference, the average total life expectancy for a 62-year-old is slightly past age 80.5.)

RULE #3 In a married couple, having the person with the higher primary insurance amount delay benefits increases the amount the couple will receive as long as *either* spouse is alive. Age 80.5 is again the breakeven point, but only one of the two spouses needs to make it to the point at which the higher-earning spouse would have been age 80.5 for it to be beneficial to delay benefits. (And, generally speaking, this makes it advantageous for the higher earner to delay benefits.)

RULE #4: In a married couple, having the spouse with the lower earnings history delay benefits only increases the monthly amount the couple will receive while *both* spouses are still alive. Naturally, this makes it relatively less advantageous for this person to hold off on taking benefits. (That said, it could still be a good idea if both spouses expect to live a long time or if the couple is particularly afraid of running out of money during retirement.)

RULE #5: Via clever planning, there is often a way for one spouse to receive a few years of "free" benefits: by filing a restricted application for just spousal benefits at full retirement age, while allowing his/her own benefit to continue growing until age 70, for example.

RULE #6: The higher the after-inflation rate of return you can earn on your investments, the better it becomes to take Social Security early and invest the money. As a result, if inflation-adjusted interest rates are very high (which, as I write this, they are not) or if you have a very high risk tolerance (because you do not expect to need your Social Security money to pay the bills, for example), you may be better off taking the money early.

Please remember, however, that these are just general guidelines. There are many factors involved in Social Security-related decisions, and depending on your circumstances, it may be best to break one or more of these rules. When in doubt, seek the assistance of a knowledgeable financial planner.

Appendix A

Widow(er) Benefits: Math Details

When a widow(er) claims widow(er) benefits prior to full retirement age, the amount he/she receives is reduced. If the deceased spouse had not claimed his/her retirement benefits prior to full retirement age, the surviving spouse's benefit will be reduced by 28.5% if he/she claims widow(er) benefits as early as possible (at age 60). And the amount he/she receives will increase from there on a pro-rata basis for each month closer he/she is to full retirement age when he/she claims widow(er) benefits.

If, however, the surviving spouse claims widow(er) benefits prior to full retirement age, and the deceased spouse *had* claimed his/her retirement benefit prior to full retirement age, the calculation is different. The starting point for the calculation is now the deceased spouse's PIA rather than the amount that the deceased spouse was receiving at death. From there, the same reduction (e.g., 28.5% if claimed at age 60) will apply. However, the resulting benefit is then limited to the greater of:

- 82.5% of the deceased spouse's PIA, or

- The amount the deceased spouse was receiving at the time of his/her death.

In other words, from the point of view of a worker, just as delaying claiming benefits *increases* what your widow(er) can collect, claiming early *reduces* what your widow(er) can collect, but not below 82.5% of your PIA. However, if your widow(er) then claims widow(er) benefits before full retirement age, the resulting amount can be below 82.5% of your PIA.

Appendix B

Suggestions for Further Reading

I wholeheartedly recommend the following books if you have a desire to do any further reading about Social Security:

- *A Social Security Owner's Manual* by Jim Blankenship,
- *Social Security for Dummies* by Jonathan Peterson,
- *Social Security Strategies: How to Optimize Retirement Benefits* by William Reichenstein and William Meyer, and
- *Social Security: The Inside Story* by Andy Landis

In addition, the *Social Security Handbook* is a useful reference when you need a thorough explanation of a given topic. Alternatively, if you ever need to look up the actual law, you can find the applicable part of the Code of Federal Regulations on the SSA website.[1]

---

[1] The *Social Security Handbook* can be found at:
http://www.ssa.gov/OP_Home/handbook/handbook.html
Part 404 of the Code can be found at:
http://www.ssa.gov/OP_Home/cfr20/404/404-0000.htm

Acknowledgements

As always, my thanks go to my editing team: Michelle, Pat, Debbi, and Kalinda. Thank you once again.

In addition, my sincere gratitude goes to Albert Kinderman and Jim Blankenship, CFP, EA for contributing their time as technical editors, as well as to the anonymous sscritic of the Bogleheads investment forum and Jewell Colbert of the Social Security Administration for taking the time to answer my questions.

About the Author:

Mike Piper is a Missouri Licensed CPA. He is the author of eight personal finance books as well as the popular blog ObliviousInvestor.com.

Also by Mike Piper:

Can I Retire? Managing Your Retirement Savings Explained in 100 Pages or Less

Investing Made Simple: Investing in Index Funds Explained in 100 Pages or Less

Taxes Made Simple: Income Taxes Explained in 100 Pages or Less

Independent Contractor, Sole Proprietor, and LLC Taxes Explained in 100 Pages or Less

LLC vs. S-Corp vs. C-Corp Explained in 100 Pages or Less

Accounting Made Simple: Accounting Explained in 100 Pages or Less

Oblivious Investing: Building Wealth by Ignoring the Noise

INDEX

Made in the USA
Lexington, KY
08 March 2013